Michelle Robertson

KETO DIET RECIPES

Yummy And Easy Recipes of Main Dishes Perfectly In Line With The Ketogenic Diet That Will Help You Achieve Your Goal of Weight Loss

TABLE OF CONTENTS

INTRODUCTION 9

COLE SLAW KETO WRAP 11
KETO CHICKEN CLUB LETTUCE WRAP 13
KETO BROCCOLI SALAD 15
KETO SHEET PAN CHICKEN AND RAINBOW VEGGIES 17
SKINNY BANG BANG ZUCCHINI NOODLES 20
KETO CAESAR SALAD 23
KETO BUFFALO CHICKEN EMPANADAS 25
PEPPERONI AND CHEDDAR STROMBOLI 28
TUNA CASSEROLE 30
BRUSSELS SPROUT AND HAMBURGER GRATIN 32
BACON APPETIZERS 34
CHERRY TOMATO SALAD WITH CHORIZO 36
CHICKEN CAESAR SALAD & BOK CHOY 38
HEALTHY ROASTED GREEN BEAN & MUSHROOM SALAD 40
ITALIAN TRI-COLOR SALAD 42
LEMON-GARLIC CHICKEN THIGHS 44
BLACK-EYED PEAS PLATTER 47
HUMBLE MUSHROOM RICE 49
SWEET AND SOUR CABBAGE AND APPLES 51
ORANGE AND CHILI GARLIC SAUCE 53
TANTALIZING MUSHROOM GRAVY 55
EVERYDAY VEGETABLE STOCK 57
GRILLED CHICKEN WITH LEMON AND FENNEL 59
CARAMELIZED PORK CHOPS AND ONION 61
HEARTY PORK BELLY CASSEROLE 63
FASCINATING SPINACH AND BEEF MEATBALLS 65
JUICY AND PEPPERY TENDERLOIN 67
HEALTHY AVOCADO BEEF PATTIES 69
RAVAGING BEEF POT ROAST 71
LOVELY FAUX MAC AND CHEESE 73
ANCHO MACHO CHILI 75
CHICKEN SUPREME PIZZA 78
ZUCCHINI PIZZA BITES 81
PORK CUTLETS WITH SPANISH ONION 83
RICH AND EASY PORK RAGOUT 85
PULLED PORK WITH MINT 87
FESTIVE MEATLOAF 90
RICH WINTER BEEF STEW 93

CRUNCHY CHICKEN MILANESE 96
SPINACH 99

CONCLUSION 103

Introduction

Why Is the Ketogenic Diet So Effective?

Some people think that the biggest reason keto is so effective is that you're cutting carbs out of your regimen and you're focusing on leaner meats and healthy fats with high-quality protein to make up the difference. I have to say; it certainly doesn't hurt your efforts.

The thing that makes keto so effective, though, really is the process of ketosis. Once your body makes that switch, it becomes so much easier for your body to access the stores of fat that have become stubborn and stuck in over the years.

However, it is vitally important that you ensure the quality of the food you're taking on is higher. You want foods that contain Omega fatty acids, you want foods that contain a lot of vitamins and minerals, and you want foods that are generally very healthy. That isn't to say that you can't have bacon and cream, but make sure you're taking on lots of greens, vegetables, fiber, and all the good stuff!

One of the most important things that you'll learn is that you need to balance your macronutrients. Macronutrients are quite simply a type of food that are required in large amounts in a diet. Typically with keto, the macros you will most commonly hear talked about are carbohydrates, protein, and fat. You want to make sure that your macronutrients are consumed not in specific amounts, but in a ratio with one another.

- **Protein** – 15%–30%

- **Fat** – 60%–75%

- **Carbohydrate** – 5%–10% (with a cap of about 15g per day)

On keto, it's not necessary to track all your calories and macros to the percent. It is helpful to know a ballpark for each of these and try to keep them in that balance. Once you get used to eating in this way, you'll be able to eyeball it, more or less.

Cole Slaw Keto Wrap

Preparation time: 15 minutes.

Cooking time: 20 minutes.

Servings: 2

Ingredients:

- 3 cups sliced thin red cabbage

- 0.5 cups green onions, diced

- 0.75 cups mayo

- 2 teaspoons apple cider vinegar

- 0.25 teaspoon salt

- 16 pieces collard green, stems removed

- 1 pound ground meat of choice, cooked and chilled

- 0.33 cup alfalfa sprouts

- Toothpicks, to hold wraps together

Directions:

1. Mix the slaw ingredients with a spoon in a large-sized bowl until everything is well-coated.

2. Place a collard green on a plate and scoop a tablespoon or two of coleslaw on the edge of the leaf. Top it with a scoop of meat and sprouts.

3. Roll and tuck the sides to keep the filling from spilling.

4. Once you assemble the wrap, put in your toothpicks in a way that holds the wrap together until you are ready to beat it. Just repeat this with the leftover leaves.

Nutrition:

- **Calories:** 409

- **Carbs:** 4g

- **Fat:** 42g

- **Protein:** 2g

Keto Chicken Club Lettuce Wrap

Preparation time: 15 minutes.

Cooking time: 15 minutes.

Servings: 1

Ingredients:

- 1 head of iceberg lettuce with the core and outer leaves removed

- 1 tablespoon mayonnaise

- 6 slices of organic chicken or turkey breast

- 2 cooked strips bacon, halved

- 2 slices of tomato

Directions:

1. Line your working surface with a large slice of parchment paper.

2. Layer 6–8 large leaves of lettuce in the center of the paper to make a base of around 9–10 inches.

3. Spread the mayo in the center and lay with chicken or turkey, bacon, and tomato.

4. Starting with the end closest to you, roll the wrap like a jelly roll with the parchment paper as your guide. Keep it tight and halfway through, roll tuck in the ends of the wrap.

5. When it is completely wrapped, roll the rest of the parchment paper around it, and use a knife to cut it in half.

Nutrition:

- **Carbs:** 4g
- **Fat:** 78g
- **Protein:** 28g
- **Calories:** 837

Keto Broccoli Salad

Preparation time: 10 minutes.

Cooking time: 0 minutes.

Servings: 4–6

Ingredients:

For your salad:

- 2 medium-sized heads broccoli, florets chunked

- 2 cups red cabbage, well shredded

- 0.5 cups sliced almonds, roasted

- 1 stalk green onions, sliced

- 0.5 cups raisins

For your orange almond dressing:

- 0.33 cup orange juice

- 0.25 cup almond butter

- 2 tablespoons coconut aminos

- 1 shallot, small-sized, chopped finely

- ½ teaspoon salt

Directions:

1. Use a food processor to pulse together salt, shallot, amino, nut butter, and orange juice. Make sure it is perfectly smooth.

2. Use a medium-sized bowl to combine the other ingredients. Toss it with dressing and serve.

Nutrition:

- **Carbs:** 13g

- **Fat:** 94g

- **Protein:** 22g

- **Calories:** 1022

Keto Sheet Pan Chicken and Rainbow Veggies

Preparation time: 15 minutes.

Cooking time: 25 minutes.

Servings: 4

Ingredients:

- Nonstick spray

- 1 pound chicken breasts, boneless, and skinless

- 1 tablespoon sesame oil

- 2 tablespoons soy sauce

- 2 tablespoons honcy

- 2 red pepper, medium-sized, sliced

- 2 yellow pepper, medium-sized, sliced

- 3 carrots, medium-sized, sliced

- ½ head broccoli cut up

- 2 red onions, medium-size and sliced

- 2 tablespoons EVOO

- Pepper and salt, to taste

- 0.25 cup parsley, fresh herb, chopped

Directions:

1. First, spray your baking sheet with cooking spray and bring the oven to a temperature of 400°F.

2. Then, put the chicken in the middle of the sheet. Separately, combine the oil and the soy sauce. Brush the mix over the chicken.

3. Separate your veggies across the plate. Sprinkle with oil and then toss them gently to ensure they are coated. Finally, spice up with pepper and salt.

4. Set tray into the oven and cook for around 25 minutes until all is tender and done throughout.

5. After taking it out of the oven, garnish using parsley. Divide everything between those prepared containers paired with your favorite greens.

Nutrition:

- **Carbs:** 9g

- **Fat:** 30g

- **Protein:** 30g

- **Calories:** 437kcal

Skinny Bang Bang Zucchini Noodles

Preparation time: 15 minutes.

Cooking time: 15 minutes.

Servings: 4

Ingredients:

For the noodles:

- 4 medium zucchini spiraled

- 1 tablespoon olive oil

For the sauce:

- 0.25 cup + 2 tablespoons plain Greek yogurt

- 0.25 cup + 2 tablespoons mayo

- 0.25 cup + 2 tablespoons Thai sweet chili sauce

- 1.5 teaspoons honey

- 1.5 teaspoons sriracha

- 2 teaspoons lime juice

Directions:

1. If you are using any meats for this dish, such as chicken or shrimp, cook them first, then set them aside.

2. Pour the oil into a large-sized skillet at medium temperature.

3. After the oil is well heated, stir in the spiraled zucchini noodles.

4. Cook the "noodles" until tender yet still crispy.

5. Remove from the heat, drain, and set at rest for at least 10 minutes.

6. Combine the sauce ingredients together into a large-sized, both until perfectly smooth.

7. Give it a taste and adjust as needed.

8. Divide into 4 small containers. Mix your noodles with any meats you cooked and add them to meal prepared containers.

9. When you're ready to eat it, heat the noodles, drain any excess water, and mix in the sauce.

Nutrition:

- **Carbs:** 18g

- **Fat:** 1g

- **Protein**: 9g

- **Calories:** 161g

Keto Caesar Salad

Preparation time: 15 minutes.

Cooking time: 0 minutes.

Servings: 4

Ingredients:

- 1.5 cups mayonnaise

- 3 tablespoons apple cider vinegar/ACV

- 1 teaspoon Dijon mustard

- 4 anchovy fillets

- 24 romaine heart leaves

- 4 ounces pork rinds, chopped

Directions:

1. Place the mayo with ACV, mustard, and anchovies into a blender and process until smooth and dressing like.

2. Prepare romaine leaves and pour out dressing across them evenly.

3. Top with pork rinds and enjoy.

Nutrition:

- **Carbs:** 4g

- **Fat:** 86g

- **Protein:** 47g

- **Calories:** 993kcal

Keto Buffalo Chicken Empanadas

Preparation time: 20 minutes.

Cooking time: 30 minutes.

Servings: 6

Ingredients:

For the empanada dough:

- 1(½) cups mozzarella cheese

- 3 ounces cream cheese

- 1 whisked egg

- 2 cups almond flour

For the buffalo chicken filling:

- 2 cups of cooked shredded chicken

- 2 tablespoons butter, melted

- 0.33 cup hot sauce

Directions:

1. Bring the oven to a temperature of 425°F.

2. Put the cheese and cream cheese into a microwave-safe dish. Microwave at 1-minute intervals until completely combined.

3. Stir the flour and egg into the dish until it is well-combined. Add any additional flour for consistency—until it stops sticking to your fingers.

4. With another medium-sized bowl, combine the chicken with sauce and set aside.

5. Cover a flat surface with plastic wrap or parchment paper and sprinkle with almond flour.

6. Spray a rolling pin to avoid sticking and use it to press the dough flat.

7. Make circle shapes out of this dough with a lid, a cup, or a cookie-cutter. For the excess dough, roll back up and repeat the process.

8. Portion out spoonful of filling into these dough circles but keep them only on one half.

9. Fold the other half over to close up into half-moon shapes. Press on the edges to seal them.

10. Lay on a lightly greased cooking sheet and bake for around 9 minutes until perfectly brown.

Nutrition:

- **Carbs:** 20g

- **Fat:** 96g

- **Protein:** 74g

- **Calories:** 1217kcal

Pepperoni and Cheddar Stromboli

Preparation time: 15 minutes.

Cooking time: 20 minutes.

Servings: 3

Ingredients:

- 1.25 cups mozzarella cheese

- 0.25 cup almond flour

- 3 tablespoons coconut flour

- 1 teaspoon Italian seasoning

- 1 large-sized egg, whisked

- 6 ounces deli ham, sliced

- 2 ounces pepperoni, sliced

- 4 ounces cheddar cheese, sliced

- 1 tablespoon butter, melted

- 6 cups salad greens

Directions:

1. First, bring the oven to a temperature of 400°F and prepare a baking tray with some parchment paper.

2. Use the microwave to melt the mozzarella until it can be stirred.

3. Mix flours and Italian seasoning in a separate small-sized bowl.

4. Put the melted cheese and stir together with pepper and salt to taste.

5. Stir in the egg and process the dough with your hands. Pour it onto that prepared baking tray.

6. Roll out the dough with your hands or a pin. Cut slits that mark out 4 equal rectangles.

7. Put the ham and cheese onto the dough, then brush with butter and close up, putting the seal end down.

8. Bake for around 17 minutes until well-browned. Slice up and serve.

Nutrition:

- **Carbs:** 20g

- **Fat:** 13g

- **Protein:** 11g

- **Calories:** 240kcal

Tuna Casserole

Preparation time: 15 minutes.

Cooking time: 10 minutes.

Servings: 4

Ingredients:

- 16 ounces tuna in oil, drained

- 2 tablespoons butter

- 1(1/2) teaspoon salt

- 1 teaspoon black pepper

- 1 teaspoon chili powder

- 6 stalks celery

- 1 teaspoon green bell pepper

- 1 teaspoon yellow onion

- 4 ounces Parmesan cheese, grated

- 1 cup mayonnaise

Directions:

1. Heat the oven to 400°F.

2. Chop the onion, bell pepper, and celery very fine and fry in the melted butter for five minutes.

3. Stir together with the chili powder, parmesan cheese, tuna, and mayonnaise.

4. Use lard to grease an eight by eight-inch or nine by a nine-inch baking pan.

5. Add the tuna mixture into the fried vegetables and spoon the mix into the baking pan.

6. Bake it for twenty minutes.

Nutrition:

- **Calories:** 953

- **Carbs:** 5g

- **Fat:** 83g

- **Protein:** 43g

Brussels Sprout and Hamburger Gratin

Preparation time: 15 minutes.

Cooking time: 20 minutes.

Servings: 4

Ingredients:

- 1 pound ground beef

- 8 ounces bacon, diced small

- 15 ounces Brussels sprouts, cut in half

- 1 teaspoon salt

- 1 teaspoon black pepper

- 1(1/2) teaspoon thyme

- 1 cup Cheddar cheese, shredded

- 1 tablespoon Italian seasoning

- 4 tablespoons sour cream

- 2 tablespoons butter

Directions:

1. Heat the oven to 425°F.

2. Fry bacon and Brussels sprouts in butter for five minutes.

3. Stir in the sour cream and pour this mix into a greased eight by and eight-inch baking pan.

4. Cook the ground beef and season with salt and pepper, then add this mix to the baking pan.

5. Top with the herbs and the shredded cheese. Bake for twenty minutes.

Nutrition:

- **Calories:** 770kcal

- **Carbs:** 8g

- **Fat:** 62g

- **Protein:** 42g

Bacon Appetizers

Preparation time: 15 minutes.

Cooking time: 2 hours.

Servings: 6

Ingredients:

- 1 pack Keto crackers

- ¾ cup Parmesan cheese, grated

- 1 pound bacon, sliced thinly

Directions:

1. Preheat your oven to 250°F.

2. Arrange the crackers on a baking sheet.

3. Sprinkle cheese on top of each cracker.

4. Wrap each cracker with the bacon.

5. Bake in the oven for 2 hours.

Nutrition:

- **Calories:** 290kcal

- **Protein:** 11.66g

- **Fat:** 25.94g

- **Carbs:** 6.84g

Cherry Tomato Salad with Chorizo

Preparation time: 15 minutes.

Cooking time: 50 minutes.

Servings: 4

Ingredients:

- 2.5 cups cherry tomatoes

- 4 chorizo sausages

- 2.5 tablespoons olive oil

- 2 teaspoons red wine vinegar

- 1 small red onion

- 2 tablespoons cilantro

- 2 ounces Kalamata olives

- Black pepper and salt

Directions:

1. Chop the onions and sausage. Slice the olives and onions into halves, and set aside.

2. Heat a skillet and add one tablespoon of oil to cook the chorizo until browned.

3. Prepare a salad dish with the rest of the oil, vinegar, onion, tomatoes, chorizo, and cilantro.

4. Toss thoroughly and sprinkle with salt, pepper, and olives.

Nutrition:

- **Calories:** 138

- **Net carbohydrates:** 5.2g

- **Protein:** 7g

- **Fat content:** 8.9g

Chicken Caesar Salad & Bok Choy

Preparation time: 10 minutes.

Cooking time: 40 minutes

Servings: 4

Ingredients:

- 4 Chicken thighs—no skin or bones

- 0.25 cups lemon juice

- 4 tablespoons olive oil

- 0.5 cup Caesar salad dressing—keto-friendly

- 12 bok choy

- 3 Parmesan crisps

- To Garnish: Parmesan cheese

Directions:

1. Prepare the bok choy in lengthwise pieces.

2. Add these ingredients to a zipper-type plastic bag; two tablespoons of oil, lemon juice, and chicken. Seal and shake the bag. Pop it in the fridge to marinate for about one hour.

3. Prepare a grill using the medium temperature setting and cook the chicken for four minutes on each side.

4. Brush the bok Choy with the rest of the oil to grill for three minutes.

5. Place the bok choy on the serving dish topped with the chicken and a spritz of dressing, cheese, and parmesan crisps.

Nutrition:

- **Calories**: 529

- **Carbs:** 5g

- **Protein:** 33g

- **Fat:** 39g

Healthy Roasted Green Bean & Mushroom Salad

Preparation time: 10 minutes.

Cooking time: 30 minutes

Servings provided: 4

Ingredients:

- 0.5 cup green beans

- 1 pound sliced Cremini mushrooms

- 3 tablespoons vegan melted butter

- 1 lemon, for juice

- 4 tablespoons toasted hazelnuts

- 2 tablespoons Butter

- 1 tablespoon Salt

- 1 tablespoon Pepper

Directions:

1. Set the oven to 450°F. Slice and add the mushrooms and green beans to a baking dish.

2. Drizzle them with butter, salt, and pepper.

3. Set the timer and roast them for 20 minutes.

4. Place the veggies in a salad dish with a spritz of lemon juice and a hazelnuts' sprinkle to serve.

Nutrition:

- **Calories:** 179

- **Carbs:** 7g

- **Protein:** 5g

- **Fat:** 11g

Italian Tri-Color Salad

Preparation time: 10 minutes.

Cooking time: 40 minutes.

Servings Provided: 4

Ingredients:

- 0.25 pounds buffalo mozzarella cheese

- 1 avocado

- 3 tomatoes

- 8 Kalamata olives

- 2 tablespoons pesto sauce

- 2 tablespoons olive oil

Directions:

1. Slice the tomatoes, avocado, and mozzarella.

2. Stack the tomatoes on a serving platter.

3. Arrange them with the sliced tomatoes, avocado in the center with olives all over it.

4. Drop the pieces of cheese over the salad and serve with a drizzle of oil and pesto sauce.

Nutrition:

- **Calories:** 290

- **Carbs:** 4.3g

- **Protein:** 9g

- **Fat:** 25g

Lemon-Garlic Chicken Thighs

Preparation time: 10 minutes.

Cooking time: 25 minutes.

Servings: 4

Ingredients

- 4 wedges lemon

- ¼ cup lemon juice

- 4 chicken thighs

- 2 tablespoon olive oil

- Pinch ground black pepper

- 1 teaspoon Dijon mustard

- ¼ teaspoon salt

- 2 garlic cloves, thinly cut

Directions

1. Before anything, ensure that your air fryer is preheated 360°F.

2. Into a medium-sized bowl, add lemon juice, pepper, salt, olive oil, garlic, and Dijon mustard. Using a whisk, combine these ingredients and set them aside for a bit. This is your marinade.

3. You'll need a large reusable bag for this part. Put your chicken thighs and the marinade inside the bag and seal it. Leave it in your refrigerator for about 2 hours.

4. Next, take the chicken thighs out of the reusable bag, and using a paper towel, dry out the marinade. Place the thighs in an air fryer basket and cook them. You could fry them in batches, if that made it easier.

5. When the chicken thighs no longer look pink close to the bone, the frying should last up to 24 minutes to achieve this, you can take them out of the air fryer. If you place an instant-read thermometer on the bone, it should read 165°F.

6. When you serve the chicken thighs, also squeeze the lemon wedges on each of them.

Nutrition:

- **Calories:** 258

- **Carbs:** 3.6g

- **Protein:** 19.4g

- **Fat:** 6g

Black-Eyed Peas Platter

Preparation time: 10 minutes.

Cooking time: 8 hours.

Servings: 4

Ingredients:

- 1 cup black eyed-peas, soaked overnight and drained

- 2 cups low-sodium vegetable broth

- 1 can (15 ounces) tomatoes, diced with juice

- 8 ounces ham, chopped

- 1 onion, chopped

- 2 garlic cloves, minced

- 1 teaspoon dried oregano

- 1 teaspoon salt

- ½ teaspoon freshly ground black pepper

- ½ teaspoon ground mustard

- 1 bay leaf

Directions:

1. Add the listed ingredients to your Slow Cooker and stir.

2. Place lid and cook over low heat for 8 hours.

3. Discard the bay leaf.

4. Serve and enjoy!

Nutrition:

- **Calories:** 209

- **Carbs:** 17g

- **Protein:** 27g

- **Fat:** 6g

Humble Mushroom Rice

Preparation time: 10 minutes.

Cooking time: 3 hours.

Servings: 3

Ingredients:

- ½ cup rice

- 2 green onions chopped

- 1 garlic clove, minced

- ¼ pound baby Portobello mushrooms, sliced

- 1 cup vegetable stock

Directions:

1. Add rice, onions, garlic, mushrooms, and stock to your slow cooker.

2. Stir well and place the lid.

3. Cook over low heat for 3 hours.

4. Stir and divide amongst serving platters.

5. Enjoy!

Nutrition:

- **Calories:** 200

- **Carbs:** 12g

- **Protein:** 28g

- **Fat:** 6g

Sweet and Sour Cabbage and Apples

Preparation time: 15 minutes.

Cooking time: 8 hours and 15 minutes.

Servings: 4

Ingredients:

- ¼ cup honey

- ¼ cup apple cider vinegar

- 2 tablespoons orange chili-garlic sauce

- 1 teaspoon sea salt

- 3 sweet-tart apples, peeled, cored and sliced

- 2 heads green cabbage, cored and shredded

- 1 sweet red onion, thinly sliced

Directions:

1. Take a small bowl and whisk in honey, orange-chili garlic sauce, vinegar.

2. Stir well.

3. Add the honey mix, apples, onion, and cabbage to your slow cooker and stir.

4. Close the lid and cook over low heat for 8 hours.

5. Serve and enjoy!

Nutrition:

- **Calories:** 164

- **Carbs:** 41g

- **Protein:** 24g

- **Fat:** 2.5g

Orange and Chili Garlic Sauce

Preparation time: 15 minutes.

Cooking time: 8 hours and 15 minutes.

Servings: 5

Ingredients:

- ½ cup apple cider vinegar

- 4 pounds red jalapeno peppers, stems, seeds, and ribs removed, chopped

- 10 garlic cloves, chopped

- ½ cup tomato paste

- Juice of 1 orange zest

- ½ cup honey

- 2 tablespoons soy sauce

- 2 teaspoons salt

Directions:

1. Add vinegar, garlic, peppers, tomato paste, orange juice, honey, zest, soy sauce, and salt to your slow cooker.

2. Stir and close the lid.

3. Cook over low heat for 8 hours.

4. Use as needed!

Nutrition:

- **Calories:** 33

- **Carbs:** 8g

- **Protein:** 12g

- **Fat:** 4g

Tantalizing Mushroom Gravy

Preparation time: 5 minutes.

Cooking time: 5–8 hours.

Servings: 2

Ingredients:

- 1/3 cup water

- 1 cup button mushrooms, sliced

- ¾ cup low-fat buttermilk

- 1 medium onion, finely diced

- 2 garlic cloves, minced

- 2 tablespoons extra virgin olive oil

- 2 tablespoons all-purpose flour

- 1 tablespoon fresh rosemary, minced

- Freshly ground black pepper

Directions:

1. Add the listed ingredients to your slow cooker. Place the lid and cook over low heat for 5–8 hours.

2. Serve warm and use as needed!

Nutrition:

- **Calories:** 190

- **Carbs:** 4g

- **Protein:** 2g

- **Fat:** 6g

Everyday Vegetable Stock

Preparation time: 5 minutes.

Cooking time: 8-12 hours.

Servings: 4

Ingredients:

- 2 celery stalks (with leaves), quartered

- 4 ounces mushrooms, with stems

- 2 carrots, unpeeled and quartered

- 1 onion, unpeeled, quartered from pole to pole

- 1 garlic head, unpeeled, halved across the middle

- 2 fresh thyme sprigs

- 10 peppercorns

- ½ teaspoon salt

- Enough water to fill 3 quarters of slow cooker

Directions:

1. Add celery, mushrooms, onion, carrots, garlic, thyme, salt, peppercorn, and water to your slow cooker.

2. Stir and cover.

3. Cook over low heat for 8–12 hours.

4. Strain the stock through a fine–mesh cloth/metal mesh and discard solids.

5. Use as needed.

Nutrition:

- **Calories:** 38

- **Carbs:** 1g

- **Protein:** 0g

- **Fat:** 1.2g

Grilled Chicken with Lemon and Fennel

Preparation time: 5 minutes.

Cooking time: 25 minutes.

Servings: 5

Ingredients:

- 2 cups chicken fillets, cut and skewed

- 1 large fennel bulb

- 2 garlic cloves

- 1 jar green olives

- 1 lemon

Directions:

1. Preheat your grill to medium-high.

2. Crush garlic cloves.

3. Take a bowl and add olive oil and season with sunflower seeds and pepper.

4. Coat chicken skewers with the marinade.

5. Transfer them under the grill and grill for 20 minutes, making sure to turn them halfway through until golden.

6. Zest half of the lemon and cut the other half into quarters.

7. Cut the fennel bulb into similarly sized segments.

8. Brush olive oil all over the garlic clove segments and cook for 3–5 minutes.

9. Chop them and add them to the bowl with the marinade.

10. Add lemon zest and olives.

11. Once the meat is ready, serve with the vegetable mix.

12. Enjoy!

Nutrition:

- **Calories:** 649

- **Carbs:** 15g

- **Protein:** 28g

- **Fat:** 6g

Caramelized Pork Chops and Onion

Preparation time: 5 minutes.

Cooking time: 40 minutes.

Servings: 4

Ingredients:

- 4-pound chuck roast

- 2 medium sized Onions

- 1 tablespoon Pepper

- 1 tablespoon of Sunflower seeds

- 2 tablespoons Oil

Directions:

1. Rub the chops with a seasoning of 1 teaspoon of pepper and 2 teaspoons of sunflower seeds.

2. Take a skillet and place it over medium heat, add oil and allow the oil to heat up

3. Brown the seasoned chop on both sides. Add water and onion to the skillet and cover, lower the heat to low, and simmer for 20 minutes. Turn the chops over and season with more sunflower seeds and pepper. Cover and cook until the water fully evaporates and the beer shows a slightly brown texture.

4. Remove the chops and serve with a topping of the caramelized onion.

5. Serve and enjoy!

Nutrition:

- **Calories:** 47
- **Carbs:** 4g
- **Protein:** 0.5g
- **Fat:** 4g

Hearty Pork Belly Casserole

Preparation time: 5 minutes.

Cooking time: 25 minutes.

Servings: 4

Ingredients:

- 8 pork belly slices, cut into small pieces

- 3 large onions, chopped

- 4 tablespoons lemon zest

- 2 tablespoons Honey

- 1 ounce parsley

Directions:

1. Take a large pressure cooker and place it over medium heat.

2. Add onions and sweat them for 5 minutes.

3. Add pork belly slices and cook until the meat browns and onions become golden.

4. Cover with water and add honey, lemon zest, sunflower seeds, pepper, and close the pressure seal.

5. Pressure cook for 40 minutes.

6. Serve and enjoy with a garnish of fresh chopped parsley if you prefer.

Nutrition:

- **Calories:** 753

- **Carbs:** 23g

- **Protein:** 36g

- **Fat:** 4g

Fascinating Spinach and Beef Meatballs

Preparation time: 10 minutes.

Cooking time: 20 minutes.

Servings: 4

Ingredients:

- ½ cup onion

- 4 garlic cloves

- 1 whole egg

- ¼ teaspoon oregano

- Pepper as needed

- 1 pound lean ground beef

- 10 ounces spinach

Directions:

1. Preheat your oven to 375°F.

2. Take a bowl and mix all the ingredients, and using your hands, roll into meatballs.

3. Transfer to a sheet tray and bake for 20 minutes.

4. Enjoy!

Nutrition:

- **Calories:** 200

- **Carbs:** 5g

- **Protein:** 29g

- **Fat:** 3g

Juicy and Peppery Tenderloin

Preparation time: 10 minutes.

Cooking time: 20 minutes.

Servings: 4

Ingredients:

- 2 teaspoons sage, chopped

- Sunflower seeds and pepper

- 2 1/2 pounds beef tenderloin

- 2 teaspoons thyme, chopped

- 2 garlic cloves, sliced

- 2 teaspoons rosemary, chopped

- 4 teaspoons olive oil

Directions:

1. Preheat your oven to 425°F.

2. Take a small knife and cut incisions in the tenderloin; insert one slice of garlic into the incision.

3. Rub meat with oil.

4. Take a bowl and add sunflower seeds, sage, thyme, rosemary, pepper, and mix well.

5. Rub the spice mix over the tenderloin.

6. Put rubbed tenderloin into the roasting pan and bake for 10 minutes.

7. Lower temperature to 350°F and cook for 20 minutes more until an internal thermometer reads 145°F.

8. Transfer tenderloin to a cutting board and let sit for 15 minutes; slice into 20 pieces and enjoy!

Nutrition:

- **Calories:** 490

- **Carbs:** 1g

- **Protein:** 24g

- **Fat:** 9g

Healthy Avocado Beef Patties

Preparation time: 15 minutes.

Cooking time: 10 minutes.

Servings: 2

Ingredients:

- 1 pound 85% lean ground beef

- 1 small avocado, pitted and peeled

- Fresh ground black pepper as needed

Directions:

1. Preheat and prepare your broiler to high.

2. Divide beef into two equal-sized patties.

3. Season the patties with pepper accordingly.

4. Broil the patties for 5 minutes per side.

5. Transfer the patties to a platter.

6. Slice avocado into strips and place them on top of the patties.

7. Serve and enjoy!

Nutrition:

- **Calories:** 560

- **Carbs:** 9g

- **Protein:** 38g

- **Fat:** 16g

Ravaging Beef Pot Roast

Preparation time: 10 minutes.

Cooking time: 1 hour and 15 minutes.

Servings: 4

Ingredients:

- 3(½) pounds beef roast

- 4 ounces mushrooms, sliced

- 12 ounces beef stock

- 1-ounce onion soup mix

- ½ cup Italian dressing, low sodium, and low fat

Directions:

1. Take a bowl and add the stock, onion soup mix, and Italian dressing.

2. Stir.

3. Put beef roast in a pan.

4. Add mushrooms, stock mix to the pan, and cover with foil.

5. Preheat your oven to 300°F.

6. Bake for 1 hour and 15 minutes.

7. Let the roast cool.

8. Slice and serve.

9. Enjoy with the gravy on top!

Nutrition:

- **Calories:** 700

- **Carbs:** 10g

- **Protein:** 46g

- **Fat:** 3g

Lovely Faux Mac and Cheese

Preparation time: 15 minutes.

Cooking time: 45 minutes.

Servings: 4

Ingredients:

- 5 cups cauliflower florets

- Sunflower seeds and pepper to taste

- 1 cup coconut almond milk

- ½ cup vegetable broth

- 2 tablespoons coconut flour, sifted

- 1 organic egg, beaten

- 1 cup cashew cheese

Directions:

1. Preheat your oven to 350°F.

2. Season florets with sunflower seeds and steam until firm.

3. Place florets in a greased ovenproof dish.

4. Heat coconut almond milk over medium heat in a skillet; make sure to season the oil with sunflower seeds and pepper.

5. Stir in broth and add coconut flour to the mix, stir.

6. Cook until the sauce begins to bubble.

7. Remove heat and add beaten egg.

8. Pour the thick sauce over the cauliflower and mix in cheese.

9. Bake for 30–45 minutes.

10. Serve and enjoy!

Nutrition:

- **Calories:** 229

- **Carbs:** 9g

- **Protein:** 15g

- **Fat:** 6g

Ancho Macho Chili

Preparation time: 20 minutes.

Cooking time: 1 hour and 30 minutes.

Servings: 4

Ingredients:

- 2 pounds lean sirloin

- 1 teaspoon salt

- 0.25 teaspoon pepper

- 1.5 tablespoons olive oil

- 0.5 medium-sized onion, chopped finely

- 1.5 tablespoons chili powder

- 7 ounces of can tomatoes with green chili

- ½ cup of chicken broth

- 2 cloves of large roasted and minced garlic

Directions:

1. Prepare the oven by bringing it to a temperature of 350F.

2. Coat prepared beef with pepper and salt.

3. Grab your Dutch oven cooker and bring a teaspoon of oil to a high temperature. Once it's ready, add in a third of your beef and cook until each side turns brown. Continue this process until all beef is brownish. Add more oil if needed.

4. Have about 1 teaspoon of oil left. Put that into the Dutch oven and use it for cooking your onion for a few minutes. Next, add in the last four ingredients and allow it to simmer in the pot.

5. Add in your beef with all its juices, cover the Dutch oven, and cook a full two hours. After the 1-hour point, stir everything. Enjoy!

Note: This recipe makes 4 servings and is good for 4–5 days. This can also be frozen.

Nutrition:

- **Carbs:** 6g

- **Fat:** 40g

- **Protein:** 58g

- **Calories:** 644kcal

Chicken Supreme Pizza

Preparation time: 25 minutes

Cooking time: 30 minutes

Servings: 4-8

Ingredients:

- 5 ounces of cooked and diced chicken breast

- 1.5 cups almond flour

- 1 teaspoon baking powder

- 1/2 teaspoon salt

- 0.25 cup water

- 1 red onion, small-sized, sliced thinly

- 1 red pepper, small-sized, sliced thinly

- Green pepper, same as red pepper above

- 1 cup mozzarella cheese, shredded

- 3 tablespoons olive oil

Directions:

1. Heat your oven to a temperature of 400°F.

2. Using a small-sized bowl and a fork, blend the flour together with the salt and baking powder.

3. Prepare your dough with the water and the oil added to this flour mixture. Prepare a space on your counter to make the dough flattened. Do what you need, but make sure the olive oil coats the surface lightly before you dump out the dough.

4. Dump out the dough. Use a rolling pin to press it out, and coat the pan with oil to avoid sticking. Once you archive the desired pizza crust shape, place it onto a baking stone or prepared tray.

5. Set the tray in the oven, and bake for about 12 minutes.

6. After taking out the pizza from the oven, sprinkle cheese onto it and then add chicken, pepper, and onion. Finally, season with pepper and salt (to taste).

7. Put the pizza back in the oven for only 15 minutes; serve warm and in slices.

Note: This recipe makes 4–8 servings depending on how you divide the pizza. This will keep for 3–4 days.

Nutrition:

- **Carbs:** 4g
- **Fat:** 12g
- **Protein:** 16g
- **Calories:** 310kcal

Zucchini Pizza Bites

Preparation time: 10 minutes.

Cooking time: 30 minutes.

Servings: 4

Ingredients:

- 4 large zucchinis

- 1 cup of tomato sauce

- 2 teaspoon oregano

- 4 cups mozzarella cheese

- 1/2 cup parmesan cheese

- Low carb pizza toppings of your choice

Directions:

1. Slice your zucchinis into small pieces, in a quarter of an inch or less.

2. Preheat the oven to 450°F.

3. Line a baking pan or tray with foil set it aside.

4. Place zucchini pieces on the pan. Top them with tomato sauce, cheese, oregano, and other low carb toppings you like.

5. Bake for five minutes, and then broil for five minutes more.

6. Serve warm.

Nutrition:

- **Calories:** 231

- **Protein:** 26.7g

- **Carbs:** 4.8g

- **Fat:** 74g

Pork Cutlets with Spanish Onion

Preparation time: 15 minutes

Cooking time: 15 minutes

Servings: 4

Ingredients:

- 1 tbsp. olive oil

- 2 pork cutlets

- 1 bell pepper, deveined and sliced

- 1 Spanish onion, chopped

- 2 garlic cloves, minced

- 1/2 tsp. hot sauce

- 1/2 tsp. mustard

- 1/2 tsp. paprika

Kitchen Equipment:

- Saucepan

Directions:

1. Fry the pork cutlets for 3 to 4 minutes until evenly golden and crispy on both sides.

2. Set the temperature to medium and add the bell pepper, Spanish onion, garlic, hot sauce, and mustard; continue cooking until the vegetables have softened, for a further 3 minutes.

3. Sprinkle with paprika, salt, and black pepper.

4. Serve immediately and enjoy!

Nutrition for Total Servings:

- **Calories:** 403
- **Protein:** 18.28 g
- **Fat:** 24.1g
- **Carbs:** 3.4g

Rich and Easy Pork Ragout

Preparation time: 15 minutes

Cooking time: 15 minutes

Servings: 4

Ingredients:

- 1 tsp. lard, melted at room temperature

- 3/4-pound pork butt, cut into bite-sized cubes

- 1 red bell pepper, deveined and chopped

- 1 poblano pepper, deveined and chopped

- 2 cloves garlic, pressed

- 1/2 cup leeks, chopped

- 1/2 tsp. mustard seeds

- 1/4 tsp. ground allspice

- 1/4 tsp. celery seeds

- 1 cup roasted vegetable broth

- 2 vine-ripe tomatoes, pureed

Kitchen Equipment:

- Stockpot

Directions:

1. Melt the lard in a stockpot over moderate heat. Once hot, cook the pork cubes for 4 to 6 minutes, occasionally stirring to ensure even cooking.

2. Then, stir in the vegetables and continue cooking until they are tender and fragrant. Add in the salt, pepper, mustard seeds, allspice, celery seeds, roasted vegetable broth, and tomatoes.

3. Reduce the heat to simmer. Let it simmer for 30 minutes longer or until everything is heated through. Ladle into individual bowls and serve hot. Bon appétit!

Nutrition for Total Servings:

- **Calories:** 389

- **Protein:** 23.17 g

- **Fat:** 24.3g

- **Carbs:** 5.4g

Pulled Pork with Mint

Preparation time: 20 minutes

Cooking time: 15 minutes

Servings: 2

Ingredients:

- 1 tsp. lard, melted at room temperature

- 3/4 pork Boston butt, sliced

- 2 garlic cloves, pressed

- 1/2 tsp. red pepper flakes, crushed

- 1/2 tsp. black peppercorns, freshly cracked

- Sea salt, to taste

- 2 bell peppers, deveined and sliced

Kitchen Equipment:

- Cast-iron skillet

Directions:

1. Melt the lard in a cast-iron skillet over a moderate flame. Once hot, brown the pork for 2 minutes per side until caramelized and crispy on the edges.

2. Set the temperature to medium-low and continue cooking for another 4 minutes, turning over periodically. Shred the pork with two forks and return to the skillet.

3. Add the garlic, red pepper, black peppercorns, salt, and bell pepper and continue cooking for a further 2 minutes or until the peppers are just tender and fragrant.

Nutrition for Total Servings:

- **Carbs:** 6.42 g

- **Calories:** 370

- **Fat:** 21.9g

- **Protein:** 34.9g

Festive Meatloaf

Preparation time: 1 hour

Cooking time: 50 minutes

Servings: 2

Ingredients:

- 1/4-pound ground pork

- 1/2-pound ground chuck

- 2 eggs, beaten

- 1/4 cup flaxseed meal

- 1 shallot, chopped

- 2 garlic cloves, minced

- 1/2 tsp. smoked paprika

- 1/4 tsp. dried basil

- 1/4 tsp. ground cumin

- Kosher salt, to taste

- 1/2 cup tomato puree

- 1 tsp. mustard

- 1 tsp. liquid monk fruit

Kitchen Equipment:

- 2 mixing bowl

- Loaf pan

- Oven

Directions:

1. In a bowl, mix the ground meat, eggs, flaxseed meal, shallot, garlic, and spices thoroughly.

2. In another bowl, mix the tomato puree with the mustard and liquid monk fruit, whisk to combine well.

3. Press the mixture into the loaf pan—Bake in the preheated oven at 360°F for 30 minutes.

Nutrition for Total Servings:

- **Carbs:** 15.64 g

- **Calories:** 517

- **Fat:** 32.3g

- **Protein:** 48.5g

Rich Winter Beef Stew

Preparation time: 45 minutes

Cooking time: 50 minutes

Servings: 2

Ingredients:

- 1-ounce bacon, diced

- 3/4-pound well-marbled beef chuck, boneless and cut into 1-1/2-inch pieces

- 1 red bell pepper, chopped

- 1 green bell pepper, chopped

- 2 garlic cloves, minced

- 1/2 cup leeks, chopped

- 1 parsnip, chopped

- Sea salt, to taste

- 1/4 tsp. mixed peppercorns, freshly cracked

- 2 cups of chicken bone broth

- 1 tomato, pureed

- 2 cups kale, torn into pieces

- 1 tbsp. fresh cilantro, roughly chopped

Kitchen Equipment:

- Dutch pot

Directions:

1. Heat a Dutch pot over medium-high flame. Now, cook the bacon until it is well browned and crisp; reserve. Then, cook the beef pieces for 3 to 5 minutes or until just browned on all sides; reserve. After that, sauté the peppers, garlic, leeks, and parsnip in the pan drippings until they are just tender and

aromatic. Add the salt, peppercorns, chicken bone broth, tomato, and reserved beef to the pot. Bring to a boil. Stir in the kale leaves and continue simmering until the leaves have wilted or 3 to 4 minutes more.

2. Ladle into individual bowls & serve garnished with fresh cilantro and the reserved bacon.

Nutrition for Total Servings:

- **Carbs:** 16.14 g

- **Protein:** 88.75 g

- **Calories:** 359

- **Fat:** 17.8g

Crunchy Chicken Milanese

Preparation time: 10 minutes

Cooking time: 10 minutes

Servings: 2

Ingredients:

- 2 boneless skinless chicken breasts

- 1/2 cup coconut flour

- 1 tsp. ground cayenne pepper

- Pink Himalayan salt

- Freshly ground black pepper

- 1 egg, lightly beaten

- 1/2 cup crushed pork rinds

- 2 tbsps. olive oil

Directions:

1. Pound the chicken breasts with a heavy mallet until they are about 1/2 inch thick. (If you don't have a kitchen mallet, you can use the thick rim of a heavy plate.)

2. Prepare two separate prep plates and one small, shallow bowl

3. On plate 1, put the coconut flour, cayenne pepper, pink Himalayan salt, and pepper. Mix together.

4. Crack the egg into the small bowl, and lightly beat it with a fork or whisk.

5. On plate 2, put the crushed pork rinds.

6. In a large skillet over medium-high heat, heat the olive oil.

7. Dredge 1 chicken breast on both sides in the coconut-flour mixture. Dip the chicken into the egg, & coat both sides. Dredge the chicken in a pork-rind mixture, pressing the pork

rinds into the chicken so they stick. Place the coated chicken in a hot skillet & repeat with the other chicken breast.

8. Cook the chicken for 3 to 5 minutes on each side, until brown, crispy, and cooked through, and serve.

Nutrition for Total Servings:

- **Calories:** 604

- **Fat:** 29g

- **Carbs:** 17g

- **Protein:** 65g

Spinach

Preparation time: 5 minutes

Cooking time: 25 minutes

Servings: 8

Ingredients:

- 2 (10-ounce) packages of frozen spinach, thawed & drained

- 1 1/2 cups water, divided

- 1/4 cup sour cream

- Oat milk

- 2 tbsps. butter

- 1 tbsp. onion, minced

- 1 tbsp. garlic, minced

- 1 tbsp. fresh ginger, minced

- 2 tbsps. tomato puree

- 2 teaspoons curry powder

- 2 teaspoons garam masala powder

- 2 teaspoons ground coriander

- 2 teaspoons ground cumin

- 2 teaspoons ground turmeric

- 2 teaspoons red pepper flakes, crushed

- Salt, to taste

Directions:

1. Place spinach, 1/2 cup of water, and sour cream in a blender and pulse until pureed.

2. Transfer the spinach puree into a bowl and set aside.

3. In a large non-stick wok, melt butter over medium-low heat and sauté onion, garlic, ginger, tomato puree, spices, and salt for about 2–3 minutes.

4. Add the spinach puree and remaining water and stir to combine.

5. Adjust the heat to medium & cook for about 3–5 minutes.

6. Add oat milk and stir to combine.

7. Adjust heat to low & cook for about 10–15 minutes.

8. Serve hot.

Nutrition for Total Servings:

- **Calories:** 121 Cal
- **Fat:** 12 g
- **Carbs:** 9 g
- **Protein:** 4 g

Conclusion

Now that you are familiar with the Keto diet on many levels, you should feel confident in your ability to start your own Keto journey. This diet plan isn't going to hinder you or limit you, so do your best to keep this in mind as you begin changing your lifestyle and adjusting your eating habits. Packed with good fats and plenty of protein, your body is going to go through a transformation as it works to see these things as energy. Before you know it, your body will have an automatically accessible reserve that you can utilize at any time. Whether you need a boost of energy first thing in the morning or a second wind to keep you going throughout the day, this will already be inside of you.

As you take care of yourself through the afterward few years, you can feel great knowing that the Keto diet aligns with the anti-aging lifestyle you seek. Not only does it keep you looking great and feeling younger, but it also acts as a preventative barrier from various ailments and conditions. The body tends to weaken as you age, but Keto helps keep a shield up in front of it by giving you plenty of opportunities to burn energy and create muscle mass. Instead of taking the things you need to feel great, Keto only takes what you have in abundance. This is how you will always end up feeling your best each day.

Arguably one of the best diets around, Keto keeps you feeling great because you have many meal options! There is no shortage of delicious and filling meals you can eat while you are on any Keto diet plans. You can even take this diet with you as you eat out at restaurants and friends' houses. As long as you can remember the simple guidelines, you should have no problems staying on track with Keto. Cravings become almost non-existent as your body works to change the way it digests. Instead of relying on glucose in your bloodstream, your body switches focus. It begins using fat as soon as you reach the state of ketosis that you are aiming for. The best part is, you do not have to do anything other than eating within your fat/protein/carb percentages. Your body will do the rest on its own.

Because this is a way that your body can properly function for long periods, Keto is proven to be more than a simple fad diet. Originating with a medical background for helping epilepsy patients, the Keto diet has been tried and tested for decades. Many successful studies align with the knowledge that Keto works. Whether you are trying to be on a diet for a month or a year, both are just as healthy for you. Keto is an adjustment, but it will continue benefiting you for as long as you can keep it up. Good luck on your journey ahead!

CPSIA information can be obtained
at www.ICGtesting.com
Printed in the USA
BVHW091057030521
606332BV00004B/483

9 781802 537154